WOODCHUCKS

WILD ANIMALS OF THE WOODS

Lynn M. Stone

The Rourke Press, Inc.
Vero Beach, Florida 32964

© 1995 The Rourke Press, Inc.

PHOTO CREDITS
© Joe McDonald: cover, page 4; © Tom and Pat Leeson: page 13;
© Lynn M. Stone: title page, pages 7, 8, 10, 12, 15, 17, 18, 21

Library of Congress Cataloging-in-Publication Data

Stone, Lynn M.
     Woodchucks / Lynn Stone.
         p. cm. — (Wild Animals of the woods)
     Includes index.
     ISBN 1-57103-093-X
     1. Marmots—North America—Juvenile literature.
[1. Marmots.]   I. Title II. Series: Stone, Lynn M.   Wild Animals of
the woods.
QL737.R68S76 1995
599.32' 32—dc20
                                                            94–47385
                                                                CIP
                                                                 AC

Printed in the USA

TABLE OF CONTENTS

MARMOTS AND WOODCHUCKS

Marmots are chubby ground squirrels whose calls have earned them the nicknames "whistler" and "whistle pig." Six **species** (SPEE sheez), or kinds, of marmots live in North America.

Marmots dig long, deep burrows in meadows. Marmots feed on greens and sit up on their hind legs to search for danger. Their whistles echo across mountain valleys.

One of the six marmot species is often called "woodchuck" or "groundhog." Woodchucks do not chuck wood, whatever "wood chucking" may mean.

This woodchuck is sitting up to look for danger

HOW THEY LOOK

Marmots look like overstuffed prairie dogs, which are also ground squirrels.

Marmot fur may be brown, gray, yellowish or nearly black. The color depends upon the season and kind of marmot.

Marmots weigh from five to twenty pounds. They have small, rounded ears, short legs and clawed feet.

Marmots that live in the North have thick fur and fairly bushy tails. Woodchucks in mild climates have much thinner fur.

Marmots are plump ground squirrels

WHERE THEY LIVE

Except for the woodchuck, marmots generally live in mountain country. They like rocky slopes and **alpine** (AL pine), or mountain, meadows.

Woodchucks are found from eastern Alaska eastward through Canada and into much of the East. Yellow-bellied marmots live mostly in the Western states. Hoary marmots live further north, from Washington northward into Alaska.

Brower's marmots live in northern Alaska. Olympic marmots are only found in Washington's Olympic Mountains. The Vancouver marmot lives only on Vancouver Island, British Columbia.

Most of the marmot tribe live in the mountains of the West

HOW THEY ACT

Marmots, except woodchucks, enjoy each other's company. They live in little "villages," or colonies, of burrows. Woodchucks are "loners."

Marmots are active by day. They spend much of their time eating or sunning themselves.

Marmots enter a deep winter sleep called **hibernation** (hi ber NAY shun) for up to nine months.

Groundhog Day each February 2 celebrates an old legend about a groundhog's shadow being a sign of weather to come.

*A hoary marmot gathers dry grass
for the sleeping chamber in its
underground tunnel*

Wearing a metal ear tag, this Vancouver Island marmot is one of the rarest mammals in the world

Hoary marmot youngsters chatter and "box" in their mountain home

PREDATOR AND PREY

Marmots live almost entirely on the plants they eat. By "mowing" the grass and flowers around their dens, they can see danger more easily.

For a marmot, danger is likely to be a hungry mountain lion, golden eagle, bear, coyote, dog, wolf or human with a gun.

Animal hunters are **predators** (PRED uh tors), and marmots are **prey** (PRAY) for them.

A marmot defends itself best by diving into its burrow. It can also swim and climb a tree if it must.

14

As a yellow-bellied marmot makes flowers into food, it remains on guard so it doesn't become a predator's food!

MARMOT BABIES

Marmot babies are born in a grassy nest in the mother's burrow. The mother marmot usually has four babies, but she may have from one to nine.

Marmots are born in the spring. They begin to explore outside the den when they are about a month old.

Marmots become adults between two and three years of age. They can live to be fifteen years old.

Baby hoary marmots play on a rock pile while mom warms herself in the sun

THE MARMOT'S COUSINS

Among the marmot's cousins are mice that weigh less than an ounce and 100-pound beavers. Marmots and their many cousins are all **rodents** (RO dents).

Rodents are gnawing mammals that share a similar kind of front teeth. Rodent's upper and lower pair of front teeth are long and narrow, perfect for gnawing.

These teeth grow throughout the rodents' lives. The animals must keep wearing their teeth down by gnawing.

The Columbia ground squirrel is a pint-sized cousin of the marmots

MARMOTS AND PEOPLE

Hunters kill thousands of hoary marmots, yellow-bellied marmots, and woodchucks each year. Marmots are considered game animals in some places and hunted only during an "open season."

In other places, marmots—woodchucks especially—are considered varmints, or pests, because of their burrows and raids on gardens. As varmints, they can be killed at any time.

Marmot fur has little value. The meat is tasty, but few hunters eat it.

Woodchuck burrows in farmers' pastures make these marmots "varmints" in some places

THE MARMOTS' FUTURE

Yellow-bellied marmots, hoary marmots and woodchucks are common animals. Woodchucks have even moved into new areas as forests and large predators have disappeared.

Nearly all Olympic marmots are safe within Olympic National Park. Brower's marmot lives in the wilderness of northern Alaska where it, too, is safe.

The Vancouver marmot is one of the world's rarest mammals. Perhaps just 300 are left. Most of them live in protected colonies.

Glossary

alpine (AL pine) — of or referring to mountains

hibernation (hi ber NAY shun) — the deep, sleeplike state in which certain animals survive the winter

predator (PRED uh tor) — an animal that kills other animals for food

prey (PRAY) — an animal that is hunted by another for food

rodent (RO dent) — any one of a large group of gnawing mammals, such as rats, mice and ground squirrels

species (SPEE sheez) — within a group of closely related animals, one certain kind, such as a *hoary* marmot

INDEX